Tyndale House Publishers, Inc., Carol Stream, Illinois

**Celebrating the Gift
of African American
Spirituals through
Expressive Calligraphy**

Timothy R Botts

with reflections by Patricia Raybon

Visit Tyndale online at www.tyndale.com.

TYNDALE and Tyndale's quill logo are registered trademarks of Tyndale House Publishers, Inc.

Bound for Glory: Celebrating the Gift of African American Spirituals through Expressive Calligraphy

Designed by Barry A. Smith

Edited by Annette Hayward

Library of Congress Cataloging-in-Publication Data

Botts, Timothy R.
  Bound for glory: celebrating the gift of African American spirituals through expressive calligraphy / Timothy R. Botts; with reflections by Patricia Raybon.
    p. cm.
  Includes index.
  ISBN 978-1-4143-5453-8 (sc)
  1. African Americans—Religion. 2. Spirituals (Songs) 3. Calligraphy. I. Raybon, Patricia. II. Title.
  BR563.N4B665 2011
  264'.2308996073—dc22

                                   2011015996

Printed in China

17   16   15   14   13   12   11
 7   6   5   4   3   2   1

Dedicated to Naomi, Miriam, and Moses

Foreword

I learned MY FIRST SPIRITUAL IN THE fourth grade. Our music teacher at Columbine Elementary School in Denver taught us "Good News, Chariot's a-Comin'," an upbeat song we sang with innocence and as much high spirit as she would allow.

She called it a "spiritual." But my parents convinced me it was the music our family sang in church every Sunday anyway. As African Americans, we claimed the spirituals as "our" music. But as it turns out, spirituals were sung all over the world—and still are.

But spirituals are important for a deeper reason. In America, enslaved Africans had no reason to sing. Especially about hope. Especially while enduring hell. As Frederick Douglass, the abolitionist and former slave, said of the timbre of spirituals, "Every tone was a testimony against slavery, and a prayer to God for deliverance from chains."

I tried not to forget that as I wrote my reflections for the beautiful artwork produced for this book by Timothy Botts. But I almost did. Thus, an early version of these reflections for Tim's 2010 gallery show, *Bound for Glory*, appeared with more facts than heart.

Then I rewrote everything. This time I tried to find voices to speak for the plain, everyday truth of these songs. I found inspiration in the African tradition of singing impromptu songs about ordinary life. But I found power in the astute way slaves borrowed their owners' Bible heroes and stories to seed their faith in a delivering God.

Then the amazing thing happened. God heard their songs. Also amazing, we're still singing them.

I'm grateful to Tim for allowing me to join him in reflecting on the phenomenon of this music. I also thank Becky Brandvik at Tyndale House for inviting me to join the project, my agent Ann Spangler for support and advice, and my husband, Dan Raybon, for reading drafts, sharing insight, and offering encouragement.

I dedicate my part in this book to Dan and to our daughters and their families, but also in memory of my parents, William and Nannie Smith, who every Sunday took me to the church where I learned the stories and words of these songs. Then, even better, they joined me in the singing. Only God could put us on this path, then help us sing to His glory all the way.

—*Patricia Raybon*

Preface

I sang NEARLY HALF OF THE SPIRITUALS included in this book when I was growing up in the youth fellowship of my church. I also remember, as if it were yesterday, Ethel Waters singing "His Eye Is on the Sparrow" on our black-and-white television.

With this new body of work, I want to celebrate the incredible gift of music that African Americans gave to the church and to the whole world. It is amazing that these people, many of them enslaved by Christian people, saw beyond their owners' hypocrisy and embraced the real Jesus. I believe these miracle songs are an example of how God can take our deepest pain and, in response to our faith, create something beautiful.

This has been the most difficult artwork I ever created. From my Western European background in calligraphy, I've tried to make a bridge to a culture different from my own. During a period of self-doubt, I heard a beautiful interpretation of an Old English Christmas carol by a black singer. That experience encouraged me to come from the opposite direction with my paints and proceed with the project.

You may notice influences from both traditional American quilts and the wonderful patterns from Gee's Bend in Alabama. I was inspired by traditional African art and writing systems, and I was influenced by some of the best urban graffiti observed on railroad cars passing by.

I hope that my use of color and movement in these pieces helps you feel both the pathos and joy of the music. The majority of the designs are written with a watercolor medium called gouache, using pens or brushes. Most of the colored papers are Canson Mi-Teintes. The painted backgrounds are prepared with acrylic paint and wallpaper paste on Arches Text Wove. I also applied gold leaf to many of the works.

I want to especially acknowledge Patricia Raybon, who has verbally expressed the depth of these spirituals more beautifully than I ever could. Listening to the music of The Fisk Jubilee Singers, Mahalia Jackson, Jessye Norman, Moses Hogan, Rollo Dilworth, and Wintley Phipps carried me through eight years of stewing, sketching, and calligraphic writing.

Our oldest son, Andy, made frames for the original art from salvaged wood molding. Hints of that significant part of the work are expertly reflected in the book's design by Barry Smith, a fellow art director at Tyndale. This company, where I have worked for almost forty years, gave me my first publishing opportunity twenty-five years ago and surrounded me with support for this current project.

It is my desire for the visual interpretations of this Spirit-filled music to continue their work of healing and reconciliation among us.

— *Timothy R. Botts*

PART ONE

The Bible Story

These miracle stories assured the singers
that God would bring deliverance.
The same songs have the power to transport
us from God's story to our place in it today.

Rock-a-My Soul

Rock-a-my soul in the bosom of Abraham,
Rock-a-my soul in the bosom of Abraham,
Rock-a-my soul in the bosom of Abraham,
Lord, rock-a-my soul.

My Lord is so high, you can't get over Him;
So low, you can't get under Him;
So wide, you can't get around Him—
You must go in at the door! . . .

His love is so high, you can't get over it;
So low, you can't get under it;
So wide, you can't get around it—
You must go in at the door! . . .

And it came to pass, that the beggar died,
and was carried by the angels into
Abraham's bosom. LUKE 16:22, KJV

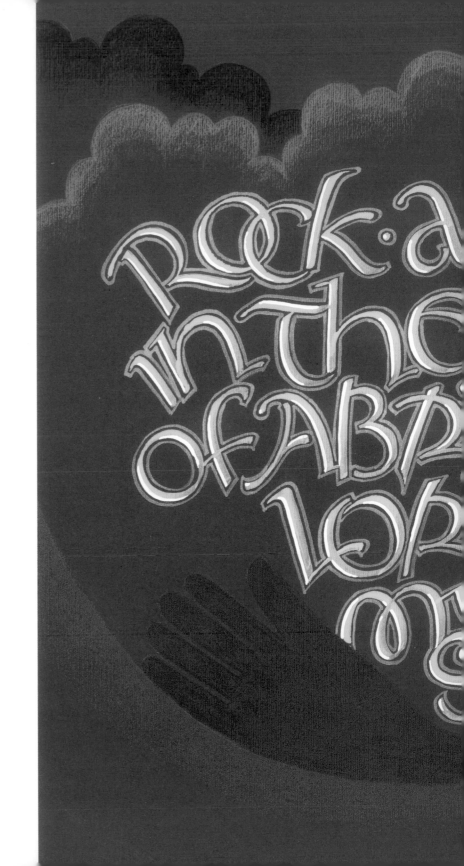

Hold me.

Tight so me and Mama and

Stella Jo and Lester and

Grammy and Lil Sis and everybody

We can't find anymore comes back home

To rest our wounded souls

In the crook of Your warm arms

Where we'll be safe again

Forever.

Together.

Cradled.

PR

Start at the bottom? Like a slave?

That's where the man and his wife put us,

Believing we shouldn't dream

Like Jacob

With pretty visions of golden angels

And a ladder so sparkly and bright

It's hard to believe it's real.

So we climb it in our dreams

Starting at the bottom.

Always reaching.

Steady rising.

Never stopping.

Then God lifts us

To the top.

PR

We Are Climbing Jacob's Ladder

We are climbing Jacob's ladder,
We are climbing Jacob's ladder,
We are climbing Jacob's ladder,
Soldiers of the cross.

Every round goes higher, higher . . .

Sinner, do you love my Jesus? . . .

If you love Him, why not serve Him? . . .

Rise, shine, give God glory! . . .

As he slept, he dreamed of a stairway that reached from the earth up to heaven.
And he saw the angels of God going up and down the stairway. GENESIS 28:12

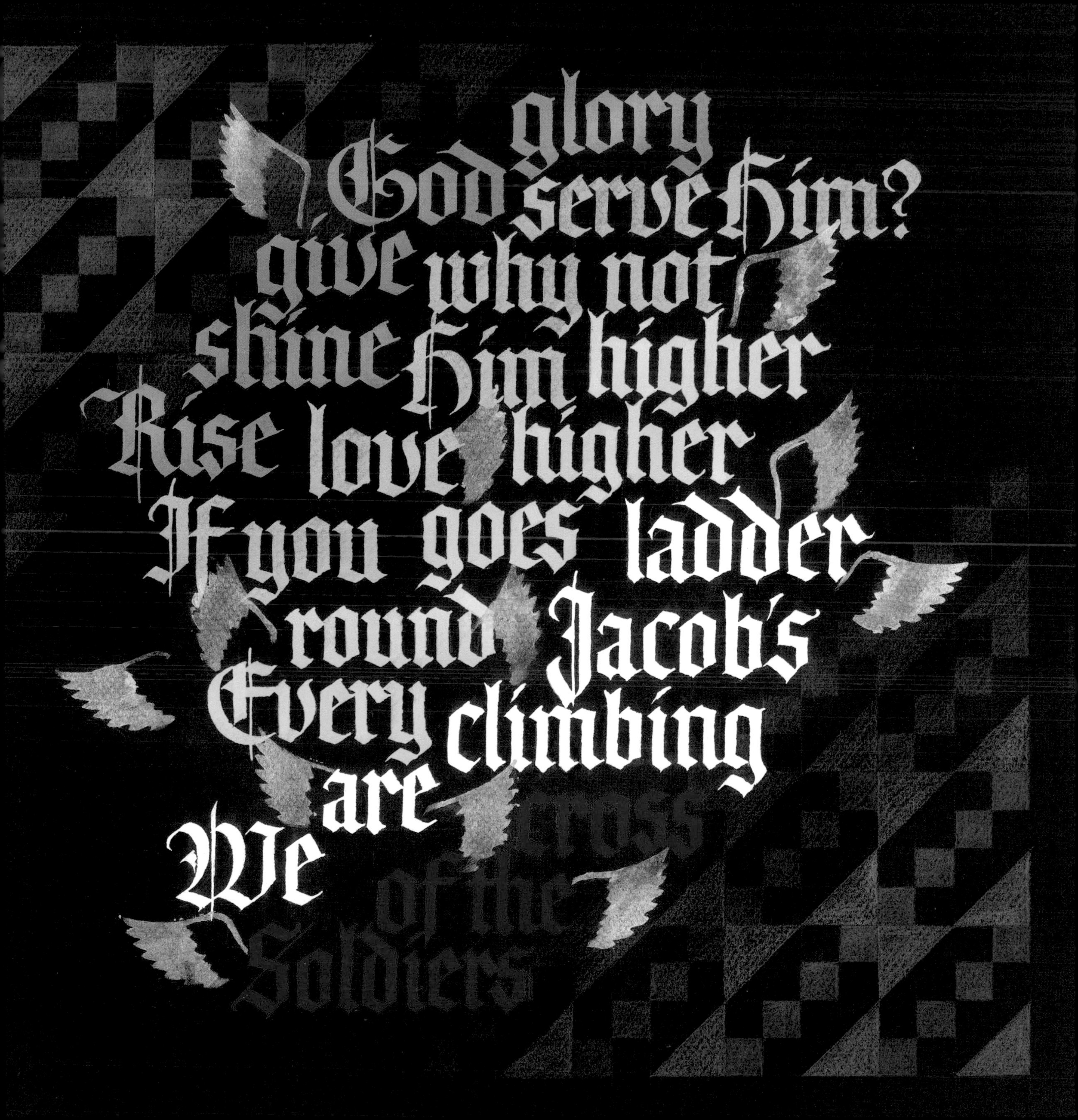

glory

God serve Him?

give why not

shine Him higher

Rise love higher

If you goes ladder

round Jacob's

Every climbing

are

We cross

of the

Soldiers

When you are called to

Take a message

To a dangerous man,

Stand close to your brother,

Feeling the heat of his resolve.

Linking your arm in his, united.

Then the dangerous man finally

Hears the truth he'll never forget:

When God's people are in chains,

Let them go.

PR

Let My People Go

When Israel was in Egypt land,
Let my people go,
Oppressed so hard they could not stand,
Let my people go.
Go down, Moses,
Way down in Egypt land,
Tell old Pharaoh,
Let my people go.

The Lord told Moses what to do, . . .
To lead the children of Israel through, . . .

As Israel stood by the waterside, . . .
At the command of God it did divide, . . .

When they had reached the other shore, . . .
They sang a song of triumph o'er, . . .

The Spirit of the LORD is upon me. . . . He has sent me to proclaim that captives will be released, . . .
that the oppressed will be set free. LUKE 4:18

Joshua Fought the Battle of Jericho

He called for trumpets,

Of all things,

To fight his foe and

Take his city,

Climb that wall,

Ford that river,

Scale his mountain,

Conquer his enemy,

Break his chains,

Inspire his army,

Win his battle

With God's brick-busting, heart-piercing,

   ear-splitting, soul-stirring

Song.

PR

Joshua fought the battle of Jericho, Jericho, Jericho;
Joshua fought the battle of Jericho,
And the walls came tumbling down.

You may talk about your king of Gideon,
You may talk about your man of Saul;
There's none like good ol' Joshua
At the battle of Jericho.

Up to the walls of Jericho,
He marched with spear in hand.
"Go blow them ram horns," Joshua cried,
"'Cause the battle is in my hand."

Then the lamb ram sheep horns began to blow,
Trumpets began to sound.
Joshua commanded the children to shout,
And the walls came tumbling down.

Joshua commanded the people, "Shout! For the Lord has given you the town!" . . .
Suddenly, the walls of Jericho collapsed. JOSHUA 6:16, 20

You may talk about
Your king of Gideon
You may talk about your man of Saul
There's none like good ol Joshua
at the battle of Jericho
Up to the walls of Jericho
He marched with spear in hand
Go blow them ram horns Joshua cried
Cause the battle
is in my hand

Joshua fought the battle of Jericho

And the walk came tumbling down
Trumpets began to sound
Joshua commanded the children to shout
and the walls came tumbling down

Little David, Play on Your Harp

Little David, play on your harp,
Hallelu, hallelu,
Little David, play on your harp,
Hallelu.

David was a shepherd boy;
He killed Goliath and shouted for joy.

Joshua was the son of Nun;
He never would quit till his work was done.

Little boy played at night,

Huddled in the hills above Bethlehem,

Watching blue sky fade to black and

Tracing the path of stars with his staff.

Then he guarded his sheep from growling creatures,

Singing softly,

Strumming gently,

Soothing his sheep,

Praising his God,

Teaching himself the best way

To take down a big giant:

Fight with Your praise.

PR

Everyone assembled here will know that the Lord rescues his people, but not with sword and spear. This is the Lord's battle, and he will give you to us! 1 SAMUEL 17:47

little
DAVID
play on
your harp
hallely
hallelu
David
was a shepherd boy
He killed Goliath
and shouted for joy

Ezekiel Saw the Wheel

Exile?

Don't mean you can't see

You're dying to get back home

Even if you can't figure out

How to get there.

So Ezekiel looked north.

Then God showed him wheels,

Turning in ways only God controls,

Reminding the prophet of God what

A prophet of God needs to preach:

A better day.

PR

(With acknowledgments to Tamara Cohn Eskenazi,
"Exile and Dreams of Return,"
Currents in Theology and Mission 18 [1990].)

Wheel, O wheel,
Wheel in the middle of a wheel;
Wheel, O wheel,
Wheel in the middle of a wheel.

Ezekiel saw the wheel of time,
Every spoke was humankind;
Way up on the mountaintop,
My Lord spoke and the chariot stopped.

Ezekiel saw the wheel,
Way up in the middle of the air;
Ezekiel saw the wheel,
Way in the middle of the air.

The big wheel run by faith,
The little wheel run by the grace of God.
Wheel in a wheel,
Way in the middle of the air.

Each wheel had a second wheel turning crosswise within it. . . .
This is what the glory of the LORD looked like to me. EZEKIEL 1:16, 28

Them Dry Bones

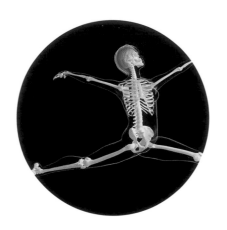

These bone-like letters are joined together and rocking in their position to suggest the music and life of Ezekiel's vision. One of the gifts of African Americans to the worldwide church is the life they bring to worship. Rarely have I heard this passage preached in all my years of church attendance, but in this song we catch the miracle of God's Spirit to regenerate us from dead-end living.

TB

Them bones, them bones, them dry bones,
Them bones, them bones, them dry bones.
Don't you hear the word of the Lord?

Head bone connected to the neck bone,
Neck bone connected to the shoulder bone,
Shoulder bone connected to the back bone,
Back bone connected to the thigh bone,
Thigh bone connected to the knee bone,
Knee bone connected to the leg bone,
Leg bone connected to the foot bone,
Foot bone connected to the toe bone.

These bones, these bones gonna rise again,
Rise and hear the word of the Lord.

I will put flesh and muscles on you and cover you with skin.
I will put breath into you, and you will come to life. EZEKIEL 37:6

It's not even a question if

My Lord delivers.

Not when I understand if

God could shut a lion's mouth,

Speak to flames,

Calm the storm of doubt and

Confusion and fear

Raging around Daniel that night,

Then God can unchain me now.

And do it fast as

Lightning.

PR

Didn't My Lord Deliver Daniel

Didn't my Lord deliver Daniel,
Deliver Daniel, deliver Daniel,
Didn't my Lord deliver Daniel,
And why not every man?

He delivered Daniel from the lion's den,
Jonah from the belly of the whale,
And the Hebrew children from the fiery furnace,
And why not every man?

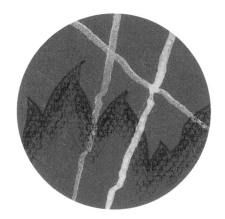

Daniel answered, . . . "My God sent his angel to shut the lions' mouths so that they would not hurt me, for I have been found innocent in his sight." DANIEL 6:21-22

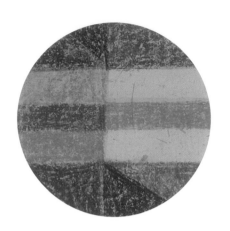

Amen

Frost on the ground

This Christmas morning.

So I pull up the quilt and

Close my eyes so I can see

The Baby Jesus

Warm in His manger,

Growing like His Father,

Teaching in the Temple,

Praying in the garden,

Dying for my wrongs,

Making things right,

Rising Easter morning

So all God's babies can prevail

Against the evils of this world.

PR

Amen, Amen,
Amen, Amen, Amen

See the little baby,
Lying in a manger,
On Christmas morning . . .

See Him at the Temple,
Talking to the elders.
How they marveled at His wisdom . . .

See Him in the garden,
Praying to His Father,
As Judas betrays Him . . .

See Him on Calvary,
Dying for our sins,
But He rose on Easter . . .

We cannot stop telling about everything we have seen and heard. ACTS 4:20

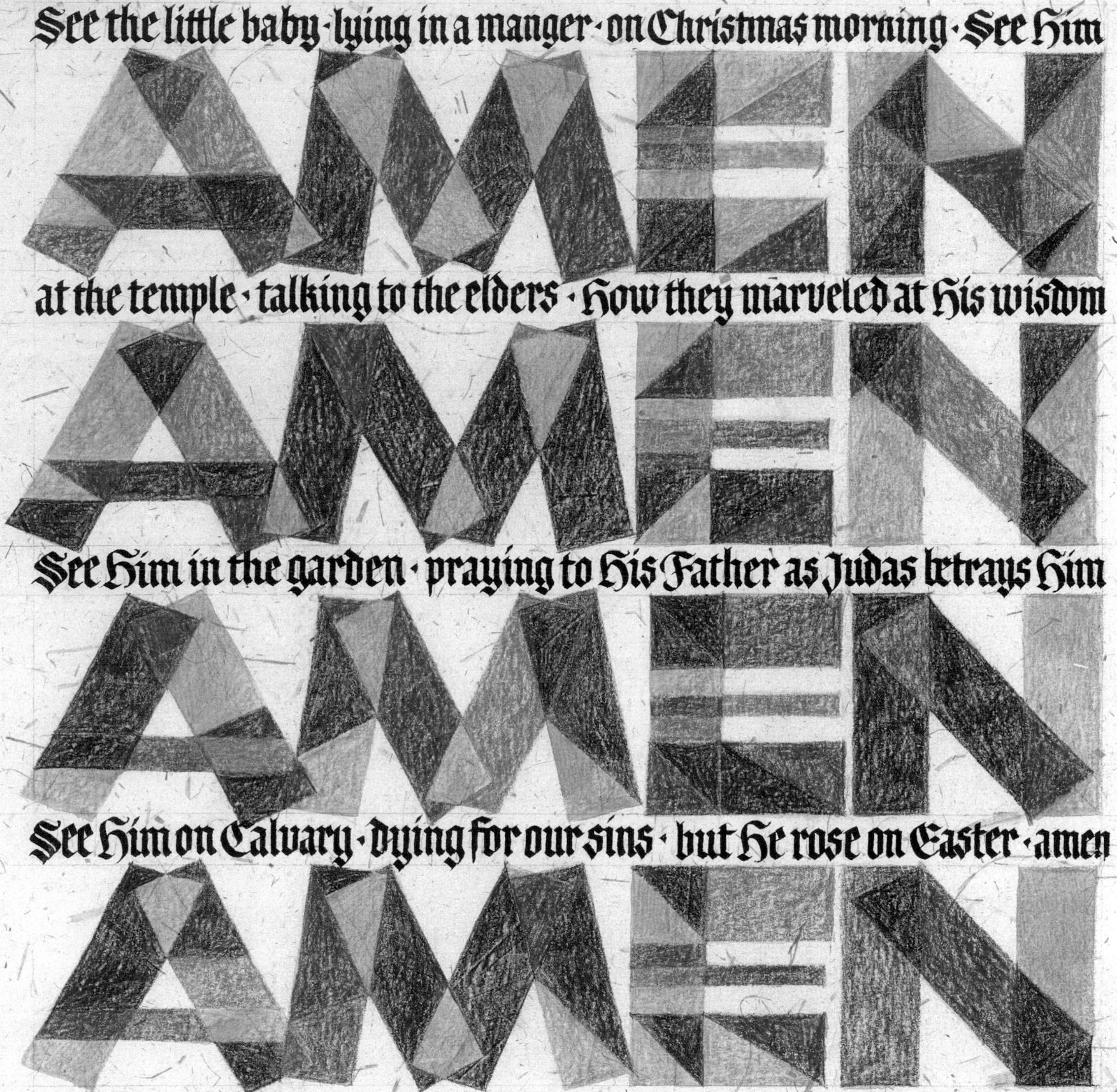

See the little baby · lying in a manger · on Christmas morning · See Him

AMEN

at the temple · talking to the elders · How they marveled at His wisdom

AMEN

See Him in the garden · praying to His Father as Judas betrays Him

AMEN

See Him on Calvary · dying for our sins · but He rose on Easter · amen

AMEN

There's a star in the east
  on Christmas morn,
Rise up, shepherd, and follow!
It will lead to the place
  where the Savior's born,
Rise up, shepherd, and follow!

If you take good heed
  to the angel's words . . .
You'll forget your flocks,
  you'll forget your herds . . .

Leave your sheep, leave your lambs . . .
Leave your ewes, leave your rams . . .

Follow, follow,
Follow the star of Bethlehem . . .

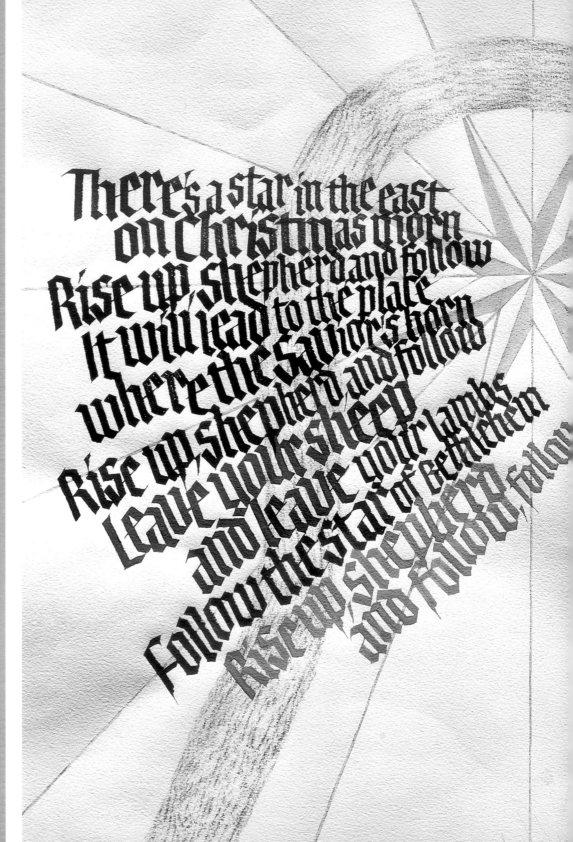

Rise Up, Shepherd, and Follow

I used the shepherd's crook to frame the star, a reminder for us not to lose our focus on the Savior. The call is for the humble to come to Christ. Those who lead need to follow. Like the star, God gives us signs along the way. This song is a call for action—there are no spectators in God's Kingdom.

TB

They hurried to the village and found Mary and Joseph. And there was the baby, lying in the manger. LUKE 2:16

Go Tell It on the Mountain

Party song!

Singing it everywhere.

In the field.

On the hills.

Sharing that remarkable,

Sublime,

Glorious,

Magnificent,

Revolutionary

Good News regarding Jesus.

He's the One who conquers our

Mountains, then promises that faith can

Move our mountains—yes, that Jesus.

He's finally here.

Now even a lonely night can be bright

Like Christmas.

PR

Go tell it on the mountain,
Over the hills and everywhere;
Go tell it on the mountain,
That Jesus Christ is born.

While shepherds kept their watching
O'er silent flocks by night,
Behold throughout the heavens
There shone a holy light.

The shepherds feared and trembled
When lo! above the earth,
Rang out the angel chorus
That hailed our Savior's birth.

Down in a lowly manger
The humble Christ was born,
And God sent us salvation
That blessed Christmas morn.

O Zion, messenger of good news, shout from the mountaintops! . . .
Tell the towns of Judah, "Your God is coming!" ISAIAH 40:9

everywhere everywhere

Go tell it on the mountain

Over the hills and everywhere

Go tell it
on the mountain
that Jesus Christ
is born

Down in a lowly manger
the humble Christ was born
and God sent us salvation
that blessed Christmas morn

The blind
man stood
by the
road
and the
cried
O Lord
show me
the way

The Blind Man

The dense letters portray our

blindness without Christ; the

gilded glasses stand for the light

He gives to those who reach out

to Him. We are all blind until the

eyes of our hearts are opened by

the great Healer, who gives us the

direction we need.

TB

The blind man stood by the road and he cried
The blind man stood by the road and he cried
The blind man stood by the road and he cried
He cried, "O Lord, show me the way, the way to go home."

The lame man sat by the road and he cried . . .
He cried, "O Lord, show me the way, the way to go home."

We all sat by the road and we cried . . .
We cried, "O Lord, show me the way, the way to go home."

Jesus sat by the road and He cried . . .
"I am the way, I am the truth, I am the life, the way
    to go home."

Jesus said to him, "Go, for your faith has healed you." Instantly the man could see,
and he followed Jesus down the road. MARK 10:52

Wade in the Water

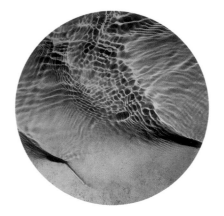

Wade in the water,
Wade in the water, children,
Wade in the water,
God's a-going to trouble the water.

See that host all dressed in white,
God's a-going to trouble the water;
The leader looks like the Israelite,
God's a-going to trouble the water.

See that band all dressed in red . . .
Looks like the band that Moses led . . .

Look over yonder, what do I see? . . .
The Holy Ghost a-coming on me . . .

If you don't believe I've been redeemed . . .
Just follow me down to Jordan's stream . . .

Why does God

Speak to waves and push back

Shorelines

And make the sea stand up like a

Sentry, stilling the salty waves

While we walk right through

On dry ground?

His Spirit gives His answer:

So He can glorify His power.

So don't just gaze at His healing blue pool.

Dive in!

PR

Sing to the LORD, for he has triumphed gloriously; he has hurled both horse and rider into the sea. EXODUS 15:21

WADE
IN THE WATER
CHILDREN
GOD'S A'GOING
TO TROUBLE
THE WATER
SEE THAT HOST
ALL DRESSED IN WHITE
THE LEADER
LOOKS LIKE
THE ISRAELITE
SEE THAT BAND
ALL DRESSED IN RED
LOOKS LIKE THE BAND
THAT MOSES LED
LOOK OVER YONDER
WHAT DO I SEE?
THE HOLY GHOST
A'COMING ON ME
WADE
IN THE WATER

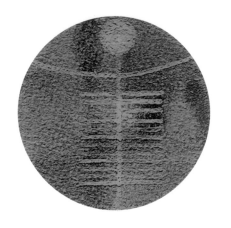

He Never Said a Mumblin' Word

Jesus went through pain, suffering, ridicule, and death—all things we try to escape—but it was His response that was most remarkable. As recorded in the book of Philippians, He didn't cling to His royal rights. How naturally the slaves must have identified with Jesus during His passion! His remarkable silence was an example to them of how to receive harsh and unfair treatment. Jesus' way must become our way.

TB

They crucified my Lord,
    And He never said a mumblin' word.
They crucified my Lord,
    And He never said a mumblin' word,
    Not a word—not a word—not a word.
They nailed Him to the tree . . .
They pierced Him in the side . . .
He bowed His head and died . . .
They crucified my Lord . . .

He was oppressed and treated harshly, yet he never said a word. He was led like a lamb to the slaughter. And as a sheep is silent before the shearers, he did not open his mouth. ISAIAH 53:7

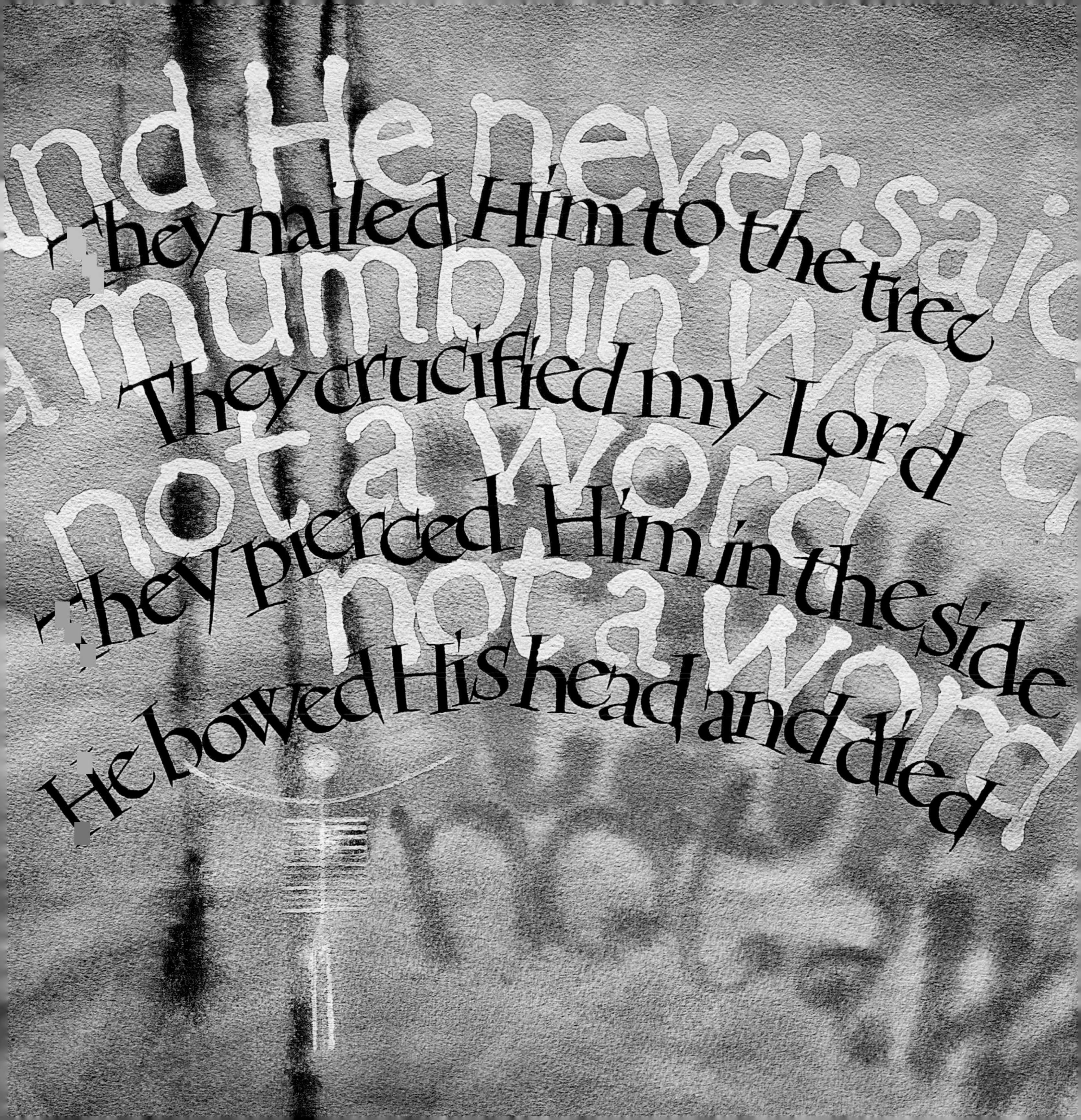

They nailed Him to the tree
They crucified my Lord
They pierced Him in the side
He bowed His head and died

And He never said a mumblin' word
not a word
not a word
not a word

Were you there when they crucified my Lord?
Were you there when they crucified my Lord?
Sometimes it causes me to tremble, tremble, tremble.
Were you there when they crucified my Lord?

Were you there when they nailed Him to the tree? . . .

Were you there when they pierced Him in the side? . . .

Were you there when the sun refused to shine? . . .

Were you there when they laid Him in the tomb? . . .

Were you there when He rose up from the grave?
Were you there when He rose up from the grave?
Sometimes I feel like shouting glory, glory, glory!
Were you there when He rose up from the grave?

Were You There?

Some folks turned and ran away,

Covering their eyes,

Refusing to watch a good man

Beat, whipped, and

Nailed with a hammer to a tree to die.

But if you

Look evil in the face

And don't fear,

Without trembling,

You finally see.

The Son rises.

PR

PART TWO
Times of Trouble

We are brought face-to-face with
the oppression and pain of those who
birthed these songs of sorrow. They became
the basis for the blues, which still speak to
our common human experience.

I Am a Poor, Wayfaring Stranger

I am a poor, wayfaring stranger
While traveling through this world of woe,
Yet there's no sickness, toil, and danger
In that bright world to which I go.
I'm going there to see my Father,
I'm going there no more to roam;
I'm just going over Jordan,
I'm just going over home.

I know dark clouds will gather 'round me,
I know my way is rough and steep,
Yet bright fields lie just before me,
Where God's redeemed their vigils keep.
I'm going there to see my mother,
She said she'd meet me when I come;
I'm just going over Jordan,
I'm just going over home.

I'll soon be free from every trial,
My body will sleep in the old churchyard,
I'll drop the cross of self-denial,
And enter on my great reward.
I'm going there to see my Savior,
To sing His praise in heaven's dome;
I'm just going over Jordan,
I'm just going over home.

Winter, for sure, is the austere season.

Still, the patterns of bare trees are starkly

beautiful and become facets for the sun

to break through. Sorrow is the universal

experience of the human race. But in

heaven the trouble will be over. It is a place

of light, and it will be safe and healthy.

TB

Hear my prayer, O LORD! Listen to my cries for help! Don't ignore my tears. For I am your guest—
a traveler passing through, as my ancestors were before me. PSALM 39:12

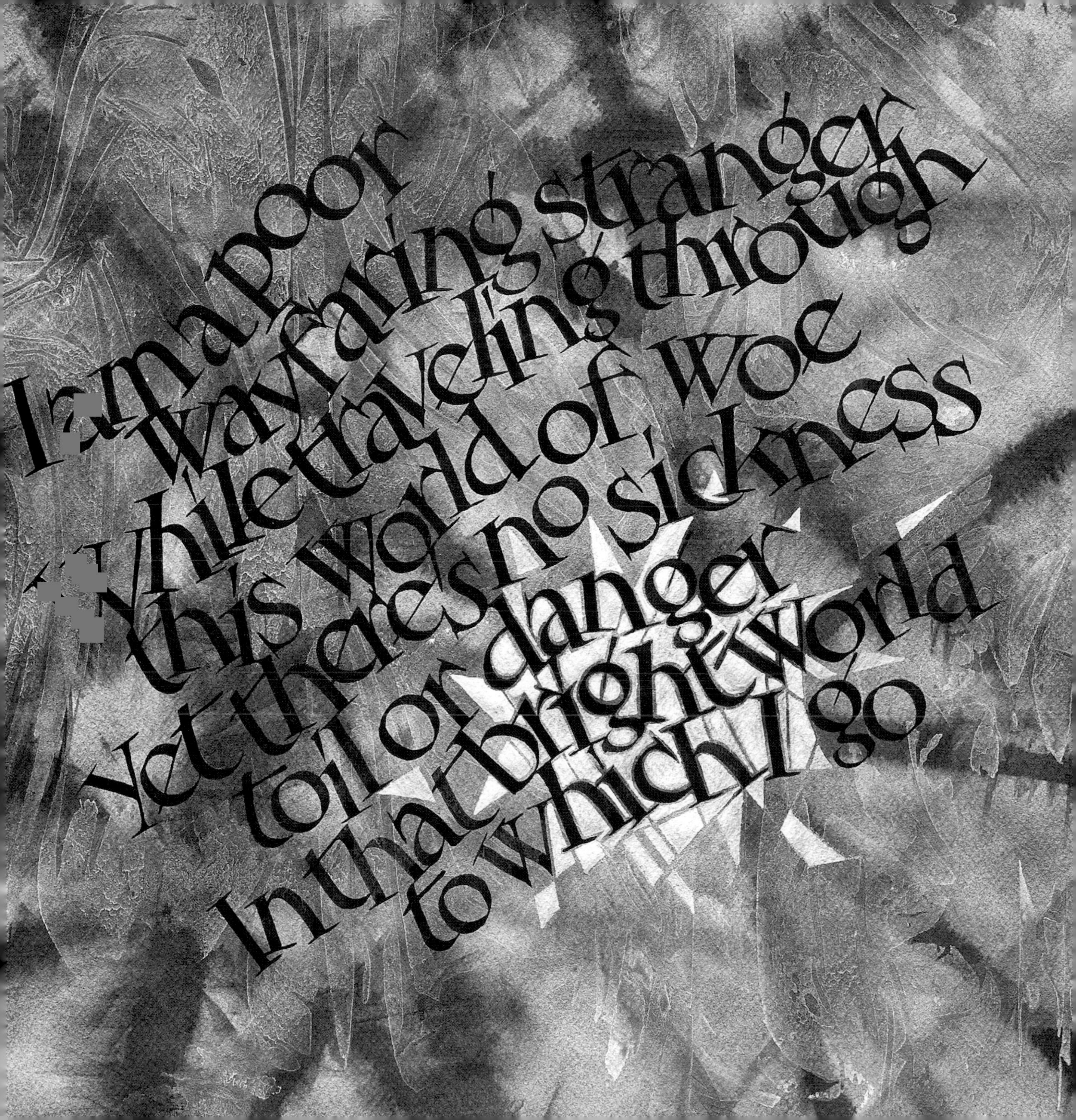

I'm a poor wayfaring stranger
While traveling through
this world of woe
Yet there's no sickness
toil or danger
In that bright world
to which I go

This was one of the most difficult pieces for me to do because I wanted so much to include the human element, but I am timid about illustrating people. I finally decided that my naive image might match the fragility of one who is suffering. Although we don't know exactly what kind of plant is the metaphor here for healing, these leaves are meant to symbolize the surrounding of the Comforter who is promised to the believer.

TB

There Is a Balm in Gilead

There is a balm in Gilead
To make the wounded whole.
There is a balm in Gilead
To heal the sin-sick soul.

Sometimes I feel discouraged
And think my work's in vain,
But then the Holy Spirit
Revives my soul again.

Don't ever feel discouraged,
For Jesus is your friend,
And if you lack for knowledge,
He'll never refuse to lend.

If you cannot preach like Peter,
If you cannot pray like Paul,
You can tell the love of Jesus,
And say, "He died for all."

There is a balm in Gilead to make the wounded whole

Sometimes i feel discouraged and think my work's in vain But then the Holy Spirit revives my soul again

sometimes
i feel like
a motherless
child
a long way
from home

The LORD is close to the brokenhearted; he rescues those whose spirits are crushed. PSALM 34:18

Sometimes I Feel like a Motherless Child

Sometimes I feel like a motherless child,
Sometimes I feel like a motherless child,
Sometimes I feel like a motherless child,
  A long way from home,
  A long way from home,
True believer,
  A long way from home.

Sometimes I feel like I'm almost gone,
Sometimes I feel like I'm almost gone,
Sometimes I feel like I'm almost gone,
  Way up in the heavenly land!
  Way up in the heavenly land,
True believer,
  Way up in the heavenly land!

The stories of slave transport from Africa to the New World caused me to ponder the huge distance of ship travel across the Atlantic. So much was lost in that voyage, and that helps us to understand the words of this extremely sorrowful spiritual. Upon seeing an image of Raggedy Andy hung out to dry, my vision for this piece became complete.

TB

Deep River

This story is when Israel crossed the Jordan on dry ground. God did this so that all nations might know His power. Sometimes it's like drowning, but going through troubles with Him will get us to the safe place. A simple rowboat enabled some slaves to find freedom in the North, but the one portrayed here has crossed oars to represent the journey finally completed.

TB

Deep river, my home is over Jordan.
Deep river, Lord, I want to cross over into campground.
Lord, I want to cross over into campground.

Oh, children, don't you want to go to that Gospel feast,
That Promised Land where all is peace?
Lord, I want to cross over into campground.

I'll walk into heaven and take my seat,
And cast my crown at Jesus' feet.
Lord, I want to cross over into campground.

Oh, when I get to heaven, I'll walk all about,
There's nobody there for to turn me out.
Lord, I want to cross over into campground.

For the LORD your God dried up the river right before your eyes, and he kept it dry until you were all across. JOSHUA 4:23

DEEP RIVER
MY HOME
IS OVER
JORDAN
LORD,
I WANT
TO CROSS
OVER INTO
CAMPGROUND
Oh, CHILDREN,
DON'T YOU
WANT TO GO
TO THAT
PROMISED
LAND
WHERE
ALL IS
PEACE?
WALK INTO
HEAVEN
AND CAST
MY CROWN
AT JESUS'
FEET

I Couldn't Hear Nobody Pray

In the valley on my knees!
With my burden and my Savior!
And I couldn't hear nobody pray,
O way down yonder by myself,
And I couldn't hear nobody pray.

Chilly waters in the Jordan!
Crossing over into Canaan!
And I couldn't hear nobody pray,
O way down yonder by myself,
And I couldn't hear nobody pray.

Hallelujah! Trouble's over!
In the Kingdom with my Jesus!
And I couldn't hear nobody pray,
O way down yonder by myself,
And I couldn't hear nobody pray.

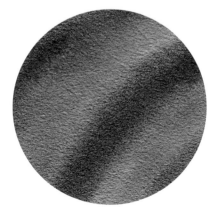

The solitude of the struggle . . .

this spiritual is a picture of the

loneliness the slave must have felt.

The appearance of our outer ear

visualizes the projection of sound

waves being received. I think these

words are a great challenge to the

church not to neglect the gift of

direct communication with our

heavenly Father who longs to

give us good things.

TB

When the Son of Man returns, how many will he find on the earth who have faith? LUKE 18:8

Listen to the Lambs

The transplanted African Americans must have felt very lost and disoriented, uprooted, orphaned, having lost direction and purpose. The Good Shepherd promises satisfaction for both hunger and loneliness. I cut the lamb design from a halved sweet potato. Unlike high-tech reproduction, the stamped images bear their individuality.

TB

Listen to the lambs all a-cryin',
Listen to the lambs all a-cryin',
Listen to the lambs all a-cryin',
I want to go to heaven when I die.

Come on, sister, with your ups and downs,
Listen to the lambs all a-cryin';
Angels waiting for to give you a crown;
Listen to the lambs all a-cryin'.

Come on, sister, and don't be ashamed . . .
Angels waiting to write your name . . .

Mind out, brother, how you walk on the cross . . .
Foot might slip and your soul get lost . . .

He will feed his flock like a shepherd. He will carry the lambs in his arms, holding them close to his heart. ISAIAH 40:11

Standing in the Need of Prayer

One of the richest examples of African art is the mask. I remember singing this spiritual often as a teenager, caught up with its rhythm rather than its meaning. So it was surprising to me years later to revisit these lyrics and make the connection between proverbial masks and our tendency to hide behind them. One of the beautiful traits of the slave musicians was their humility, an essential ingredient to entering God's Kingdom.

TB

It's me, it's me, it's me, oh Lord,
Standing in the need of prayer.
It's me, it's me, it's me, oh Lord,
Standing in the need of prayer.

Not my mother, not my father, but it's me, oh Lord . . .

Not my brother, not my sister, but it's me, oh Lord . . .

Not the preacher, not the deacon, but it's me, oh Lord . . .

Not my neighbor, not the stranger, but it's me, oh Lord . . .

The tax collector stood at a distance and dared not even lift his eyes to heaven as he prayed. Instead, he beat his chest in sorrow, saying, "O God, be merciful to me, for I am a sinner." LUKE 18:13

Nobody Knows the Trouble I've Seen

Nobody knows the trouble I've seen,
Nobody knows but Jesus.
Nobody knows the trouble I've seen,
Glory, hallelujah!

Sometimes I'm up, sometimes I'm down,
Oh, yes, Lord.
Sometimes I'm almost to the ground,
Oh, yes, Lord.

Although you see me going along so . . .
I have my troubles here below . . .

One day when I was walking along . . .
The elements opened, and His love came down . . .

I never shall forget that day . . .
When Jesus washed my sins away . . .

Why hide

When God knows everything about you

Anyway?

So He understands

Deep hurt

And a bruised body

And the pain of hunger and the sting of sorrow when

Folks betray you and leave you

Alone in the world to die.

And here's the reason He knows:

He's been there, too.

PR

For our present troubles are small and won't last very long.
Yet they produce for us a glory that vastly outweighs them and will last forever! 2 CORINTHIANS 4:17

NOBODY
KNOWS
THE TROUBLE
I'VE SEEN
NOBODY KNOWS
BUT JESUS
SOMETIMES I'M UP
SOMETIMES
I'M DOWN
SOMETIMES
I'M ALMOST
TO THE
GROUND
Glory
Hallelujah

I Want Jesus to Walk with Me

I want Jesus to walk with me,
All along my pilgrim journey,
Lord, I want Jesus to walk with me.

In my trials, Lord, walk with me
When the shades of life are falling,
Lord, I want Jesus to walk with me.

In my sorrow, Lord, walk with me,
When my heart is aching,
Lord, I want Jesus to walk with me.

In my troubles, Lord, walk with me
When my life becomes a burden,
Lord, I want Jesus to walk with me.

It's always easier to go through hard times with a friend than alone. The hymn by Joseph Scriven comes to mind: "What a Friend We Have in Jesus." The foot is not the most attractive image to many people, but it represents to me both a vulnerability and willingness to "get dirty" for a friend.

TB

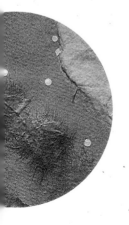

Even when I walk through the darkest valley, I will not be afraid, for you are close beside me. PSALM 23:4

I want Jesus to walk with me all along my pilgrim journey
In my sorrow · Lord · walk with me
When my heart is aching; walk with me

Steal Away to Jesus

Steal away, steal away,
Steal away to Jesus!
Steal away, steal away home,
I ain't got long to stay here.

My Lord, He calls me,
He calls me by the thunder;
The trumpet sounds within-a my soul,
I ain't got long to stay here.

Green trees a-bending,
Poor sinners stand a-trembling;
The trumpet sounds within-a my soul,
I ain't got long to stay here.

Tombstones are bursting,
Poor sinners stand a-trembling;
The trumpet sounds within-a my soul
I ain't got long to stay here.

My Lord calls me,
He calls me by the lightning;
The trumpet sounds within-a my soul,
I ain't got long to stay here.

Not afraid tonight

To let this song pass my lips.

So tonight I'll just

Sing it.

Moan it.

Cry it.

Whisper it.

Sew it on a quilt and

Hang it on the north fence to dry.

Either way don't matter since the words

Still trumpet the same thing to

Every soul longing for freedom:

Jesus is home.

So run to Him

Tonight.

PR

How quickly I would escape—far from this wild storm of hatred. PSALM 55:8

His Eye Is on the Sparrow

Why should I feel discouraged

When every bird in the sky and

Every flower on the road and

Every hair on my head and

Every song in my mouth

All remind me

That God's eye, when you stand back

And think about it,

Sees Christ in me?

And in you.

So let's sing together.

PR

Why should I feel discouraged,
Why should the shadows come,
Why should my heart be lonely,
And long for heaven and home,
When Jesus is my portion?
My constant friend is He;
His eye is on the sparrow,
And I know He watches me.
His eye is on the sparrow,
And I know He watches me.

I sing because I'm happy,
I sing because I'm free,
For His eye is on the sparrow,
And I know He watches me.

You are more valuable to God than a whole flock of sparrows. MATTHEW 10:31

I Shall Not Be Moved

I shall not be, I shall not be moved,
I shall not be, I shall not be moved.
Like a tree planted by the water,
I shall not be moved.

King Jesus is our captain . . .

The church of God is marching . . .

When my burden's heavy . . .

When my cross is heavy . . .

Don't let the world deceive you . . .

If my friends forsake me . . .

The baobab tree, native to Africa, is one of my most memorable images of visiting South Africa. With a trunk sometimes wider than its height, it was the inspiration for me of being immovable. There is a constant struggle between the forces of good and evil in our lives. The tree anchored by its roots suggests a promise of strength and stability as we take in the words of life.

TB

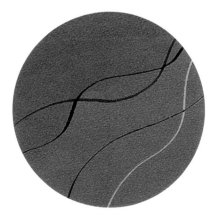

Christ will make his home in your hearts as you trust in him.
Your roots will grow down into God's love and keep you strong. EPHESIANS 3:17

PART THREE

True Testimony

Reaching out to Jesus, these people became God's children and couldn't contain their joy. Their witness bears the truth that we can move from alienation to community by the power of His love.

He's Got the Whole World in His Hands

How big is God?

Tall enough to create a world and hold it.

Wide enough to form the sky and light it.

Deep enough to create

A baby and, when it gets sold

Away and lost, never to be seen again

By its mama and the rest of us,

God's big enough to keep holding

That baby close to Him anyway,

Somehow.

PR

He's got the whole world in His hands.
He's got the big, round world in His hands.
He's got the whole world in His hands.
He's got the whole world in His hands.

He's got the wind and the rain in His hands . . .

He's got the tiny little baby in His hands . . .

He's got you and me, sister, in His hands . . .

He's got you and me, brother, in His hands . . .

Where were you when I laid the foundations of the earth? Tell me, if you know so much. JOB 38:4

○ Happy Day

This spiritual has its roots in an eighteenth-
century hymn by Philip Doddridge and was
revived as a spiritual in a number one song
by the Edwin Hawkins Singers across the
United States in 1969. The design features a
banjo, which is almost always associated with
happy music. The song captures so powerfully
the joy of forgiven sin that, whenever I hear it,
I have to join in the dance!

TB

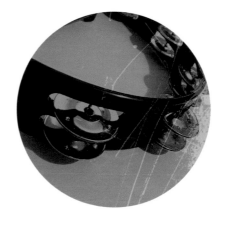

O happy day,
O happy day,
When Jesus washed,
O when He washed,
When Jesus washed,
Washed all my sins away.
O happy day!

He taught me how to watch and pray
And live rejoicing every day.

Have your sins washed away by calling
on the name of the Lord. ACTS 22:16

Lord, I Want to Be a Christian

Lord, I want to be a Christian
In-a-my heart, in-a-my heart.
Lord, I want to be a Christian
In-a-my heart.

Lord, I want to be more holy
In-a-my heart, in-a-my heart . . .

I don't want to be like Judas
In-a-my heart, in-a-my heart . . .

Lord, I want to be like Jesus
In-a-my heart, in-a-my heart . . .

I could call myself a

Christian.

But if I do,

I have to love you.

So I'll call myself a

Christian.

Then I'll give my heart to Christ,

Following in His steps,

Taking up His cross,

Learning to walk His Way,

Giving Him my mind,

So He can change me

Inside out.

PR

I will give them singleness of heart and put a new spirit within them. I will take away their stony, stubborn heart and give them a tender, responsive heart. EZEKIEL 11:19

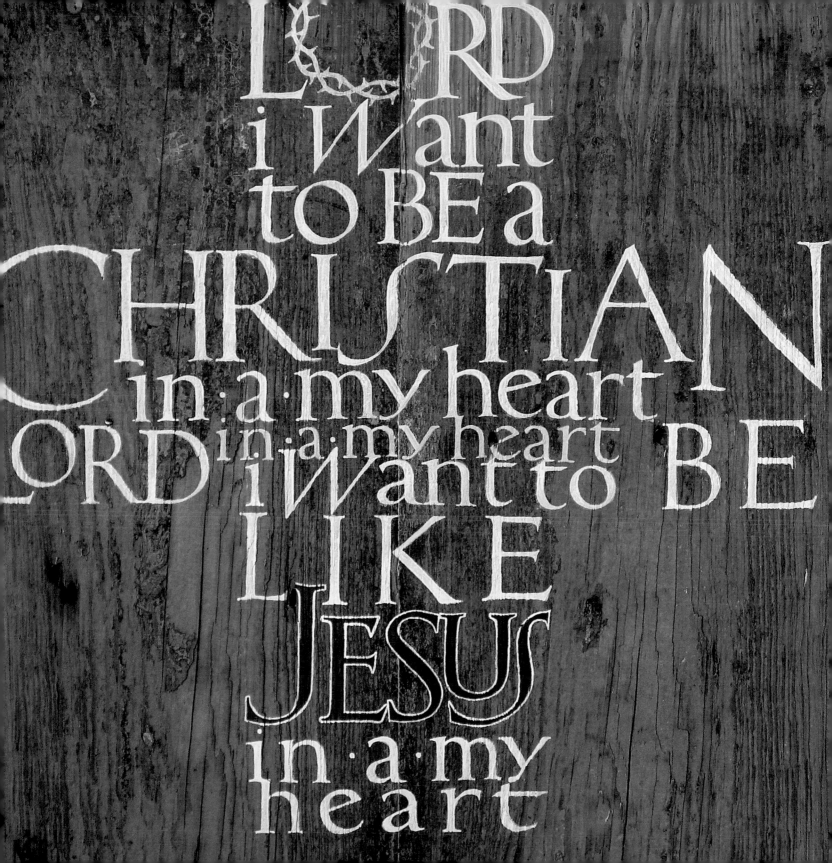

WHO'LL BE A WITNESS FOR MY LORD?

MY SOUL IS A WITNESS FOR MY LORD

Who'll Be a Witness for My Lord?

My soul is a witness for my Lord.

You read in the Bible and you understand,
Samson was the strongest man;
Samson went out at-a one time,
And he killed about a thousand of the Philistine.
Delilah fooled Samson, this-a we know,
For the Holy Bible tells us so;
She shaved off his head just as clean as your hand,
And his strength became the same as any natural man.
O, Samson was a witness for my Lord.

O, who'll be a witness for my Lord?
My soul is a witness for my Lord.

Unlike most people, I enjoy being

stopped by a freight train so that I can

study the boxcar graffiti as it passes by.

Some of the taggers are very gifted artists

whose work seems to shout for attention.

With equal passion I want my work to testify

to the grace of the gospel, which requires

a balance between expression and legibility.

TB

Live clean, innocent lives as children of God, shining like bright lights
in a world full of crooked and perverse people. PHILIPPIANS 2:15

Give Me Jesus

In the morning when I rise,
In the morning when I rise,
In the morning when I rise,
Give me Jesus.

Dark midnight was my cry . . .
Give me Jesus.

When I come to die . . .
Give me Jesus.

You may have all this world,
Give me Jesus.

Dark morning is cold

So I beg for hot

Porridge and a warm shirt,

A sweet portion of bread and a kind bit of

Mercy. I even dream

Of flying back to where I

Came from. Or hope for a

Day of justice.

Or I could turn to the

Rising Sun and ask Him

To keep me warm

All day.

PR

Yes, everything else is worthless when compared with the infinite value of knowing Christ Jesus my Lord.
For his sake I have discarded everything else, counting it all as garbage, so that I could gain Christ. PHILIPPIANS 3:8

Every Time I Feel the Spirit

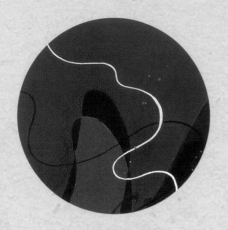

Every time I feel the Spirit movin' in my
    heart, I will pray,
Every time I feel the Spirit movin' in my
    heart, I will pray.

Upon the mountain my Lord spoke,
Out of His mouth came fire and smoke;
All around me looks so fine,
Asked my Lord if all was mine.

Jordan River is chilly and cold,
Chills the body but not the soul.
Ain't but one train on this track
Runs to heaven and right back.

Massa and his wife

Don't like that

Ring-shout music.

All that shouting and clapping and

Stomping and holy dancing,

Stirring up red dirt and dust

All over the front yard.

But every time I shout and sing

And clap my hands to glory,

Feeling my God's Spirit,

I can't help myself.

Gotta pray, too.

PR

We don't know what God wants us to pray for. But the Holy Spirit prays for us
with groanings that cannot be expressed in words. ROMANS 8:26

Commune with me, Jesus,

Making me one

With Your body,

With Your blood,

With Your suffering,

With the others

Singing down yonder

In our hiding place where

We fall on our knees,

Worshiping together the God

Who will free each one of us

While we praise Him.

PR

LET US PRAISE GOD TOGET

LET US DRINK WINE TOGETHER

LET US BREAK BREAD

WHEN I FALL ON MY KN

WITH MY FACE TO T

O LORD HA

Let Us Break Bread Together

Let us break bread together on our knees.
Let us break bread together on our knees.
When I fall on my knees,
With my face to the rising sun,
O Lord, have mercy on me.

Let us drink wine together on our knees . . .

Let us praise God together on our knees . . .

They worshiped together at the Temple each day, met in homes for the Lord's Supper, and shared their meals with great joy and generosity—all the while praising God. ACTS 2:46-47

Somebody's Knockin' at Your Door

Somebody's knockin' at your door,
Somebody's knockin' at your door;
O sinner, why don't you answer?
Somebody's knockin' at your door.

Knocks like Jesus,
Somebody's knockin' at your door,
Knocks like Jesus,
Somebody's knockin' at your door;
O sinner, why don't you answer?
Somebody's knockin' at your door.

Can't you hear Him? . . .

Answer Jesus . . .

Jesus calls you . . .

Can't you trust Him? . . .

Like a drumbeat, the outlines of the letters reverberate. Jesus' invitation is universal and generous. It is persistent, but not impolite. The fact that so many people fail to answer reminds me that only God's Spirit enables us to respond.

TB

Look! I stand at the door and knock. If you hear my voice and open the door, I will come in. REVELATION 3:20

Don't You Let Nobody Turn You Around

Through the years, despite my continuing love of letterforms, I have learned that people respond most to images. Consequently, I often try to design the words to form an element in a picture—in this case, an arrow in pursuit of a target. The goal of heaven is represented by this African-style cross, rendered in gold leaf, which never tarnishes.

TB

Don't you let nobody turn you around,
Turn you around, turn you around;
Don't you let nobody turn you around;
Keep the straight and narrow way.

I say that I'm gonna hold out,
Hold out, hold out;
I say that I'm gonna hold out,
Until my change comes.

I promised the Lord that I would hold out,
Hold out, hold out;
I promised the Lord that I would hold out;
I'm gonna wait until my change comes.

Let us run with endurance the race God has set before us . . . by keeping our eyes on Jesus, the champion who initiates and perfects our faith. HEBREWS 12:1-2

This Little Light of Mine

This little light of mine, I'm going to let it shine.
This little light of mine, I'm going to let it shine.
This little light of mine, I'm going to let it shine,
Let it shine, let it shine, let it shine.

Down in my heart, I'm going to let it shine . . .

All in my house, I'm going to let it shine . . .

Everywhere I go, I'm going to let it shine . . .

Out in the dark, I'm going to let it shine . . .

All through the night, I'm going to let it shine . . .

Jesus gave it to me, I'm going to let it shine . . .

Here is a determination to live for Jesus, not to be ashamed of Him. It is a reminder that though a single light is small, its impact is great on the darkness. Although this is often considered to be a children's song, Jesus told us that becoming like little children is a prerequisite to entering God's heaven. I enjoy the parallels between music and visual art. One of them here is the repetition of words that bolster our faith as we read or sing them.

TB

Let your good deeds shine out for all to see, so that everyone will praise your heavenly Father. MATTHEW 5:16

Down by the Riverside

Goin' to lay down my burden,
Down by the riverside,
Down by the riverside,
Down by the riverside.
Goin' to lay down my burden,
Down by the riverside.

Ain't goin' to study war no more,
Ain't goin' to study war no more,
I ain't goin' to study war no more,
Study war no more,
Ain't goin' to study war no more.

Goin' to lay down my sword and shield . . .

I'm goin' to put on my long white robe . . .

Goin' to talk to the Prince of Peace . . .

The LORD will mediate between nations and will
settle international disputes. They will hammer their swords
into plowshares and their spears into pruning hooks.
Nation will no longer fight against nation,
nor train for war anymore. ISAIAH 2:4

SHiELD DOWN BY THE SiDE

ain't goin'

war no more

to THE PRiNCE OF PEACE

Took me a while

To decide

To lay down my hurt,

My rage, my shame,

At wrapping my soul in

Hand-me-down rags

Every miserable, endless season.

But tonight?

I'll cross a river of hope,

Put on my long white robe of peace,

My dressing of grace

Outshining the ragged gall

And naked sting

Of our captivity.

PR

Keep your hand on that plow

If you want to get to heaven: Let me tell you how

Just keep your hand on the gospel plow

If that plow stays in your hand

It'll land you straight in the promised land

Hold On to That Plow

Keep your hand on that plow!
Hold on!
Keep your hand right on that plow!
Hold on!

If you want to get to heaven, let me tell you how—
Just keep your hand on the gospel plow . . .

If that plow stays in your hand,
It'll land you straight in the Promised Land . . .

The Scripture and this song both teach us to be faithful in our daily responsibilities. Our responsibilities may seem confining, but they result in prosperity in this life—and heavenly reward in the next. This design is dedicated to my father-in-law, a farmer whose straight rows exemplify his journey with the Savior.

TB

E THEY

OU W
HOW LOUD

THEM MARCHIN
FIGHTING UP

YOU W
PEALS OF

THEY LIVE WITH

he Lord in He
goin' to ansu

ice at

I went

but I didn't

nk Goa

My sou

PART FOUR

Heaven Bound

This final group of songs helps us in our constant denial to face our mortality. They provide the confidence that all God's saints will continue these songs on golden streets in freedom and fairness forever.

I Want to Be Ready

I want to be ready,
I want to be ready,
I want to be ready
To walk in Jerusalem just like John.

O John, O John, what do you say?
Walk in Jerusalem just like John,
That I'll be there at the coming day,
Walk in Jerusalem just like John.

John said the city was just foursquare . . .
And he declared he'd meet me there . . .

When Peter was preaching at Pentecost, . . .
He was endowed with the Holy Ghost . . .

Rollo Dilworth's haunting rendition of this spiritual turns the text into a question repeated over and over: "Are you ready?" Jesus' parable of the wise and foolish virgins also came to mind, for only half of them had their lamps lit. The apostle John writes that his revelation of heaven is for the purpose of blessing the church. "Come, Lord Jesus, quickly" to end all sorrow and injustice.

TB

Keep watch! For you do not know the day
or hour of my return. MATTHEW 25:13

Swing Low, Sweet Chariot

Swing low, sweet chariot,
Comin' for to carry me home.
Swing low, sweet chariot,
Comin' for to carry me home.

I looked over Jordan, and what did I see? . . .
A band of angels comin' after me . . .

If you get there before I do . . .
Tell all my friends I'm comin' too . . .

I'm sometimes up, I'm sometimes down . . .
But still my soul feels heavenly bound . . .

Oklahoma man wrote this song,

Never to imagine

We still sing it,

Still believing,

Still dreaming of traveling

In high style.

Flags flying.

Saints dancing.

Angels praising.

Making so much noise that

Jesus knows for certain

Who's crossing over next.

PR

As they were walking along and talking, suddenly a chariot of fire appeared, drawn by horses of fire. It drove between the two men, separating them, and Elijah was carried by a whirlwind into heaven. 2 KINGS 2:11

SWING LOW
SWEET CHARIOT
COMIN' FOR TO
CARRY ME HOME

I LOOKED OVER JORDAN AND WHAT DID I SEE
A BAND OF ANGELS COMIN' AFTER ME
IF YOU GET THERE BEFORE I DO
TELL ALL MY FRIENDS I'M COMIN' TOO

The Gospel Train's a-Comin'

The Gospel train's a-comin'
I hear it just at hand,
I hear the car wheels moving,
And rumbling through the land.

Get on board, little children,
Get on board, little children,
Get on board, little children,
There's room for many-a more.

The fare is cheap and all can go,
The rich and poor are there.
No second class aboard this train,
No difference in the fare.

Don't cost nothing to dream

About escape.

So I sneak out to the field,

Lay quiet in the corn

While I gaze up at heaven,

Amazed the

North Star never stops shining

Because God put it there

To lead all of us

Home.

PR

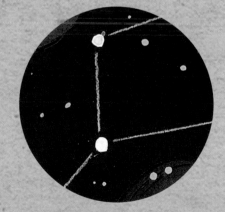

Is anyone thirsty? Come and drink—even if you have no money!
Come, take your choice of wine or milk—it's all free! ISAIAH 55:1

Soon-a Will Be Done

Soon-a will be done with the troubles of de world,
Troubles of the world, de troubles of the world,
Soon-a will be done with de troubles of de world,
Goin' home to live with God.

No more weepin' 'n' a-wailin' . . .
I'm goin' to live with God.

I want to meet my mother . . .
I'm goin' to live with God.

I want to meet my Jesus . . .
I'm goin' to live with God.

Weep and wail?

Not if you're done

With the worst life dishes out.

So you leave it.

Just pick up your soul and

Turn your back on dangerous days

And threadbare nights and

So much heartbreak and wrong and shame there's no way

To even talk about it.

So you pick up yourself and leave it. And just look at that.

When you turn your back on trouble and

War and sorrow, who

Do we see waiting up ahead

For you?

The Prince of Peace.

PR

Those who have been ransomed by the LORD will return. They will enter Jerusalem singing, crowned with everlasting joy. Sorrow and mourning will disappear, and they will be filled with joy and gladness. ISAIAH 35:10

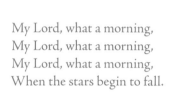

My Lord, What a Morning

As terrible as the slaves' oppression was, even more horrific is the end-times description of judgment: falling stars, blood-red moon, sun turned dark, the sky rolled up. As a metaphor for this confused state, I mixed up the traditional thick and thin weights of the letters. I chose to emphasize the singer's affirmation of faith: looking to my God's right hand.

TB

My Lord, what a morning,
My Lord, what a morning,
My Lord, what a morning,
When the stars begin to fall.

You'll hear the trumpet sound
To wake the nations underground.
Looking to my God's right hand,
When the stars begin to fall.

You'll hear the sinner moan,
To wake the nations underground . . .

You'll hear the Christian shout,
To wake the nations underground . . .

I saw a door standing open in heaven, and the same voice I had heard before spoke to me like a trumpet blast. The voice said, "Come up here, and I will show you what must happen after this." REVELATION 4:1

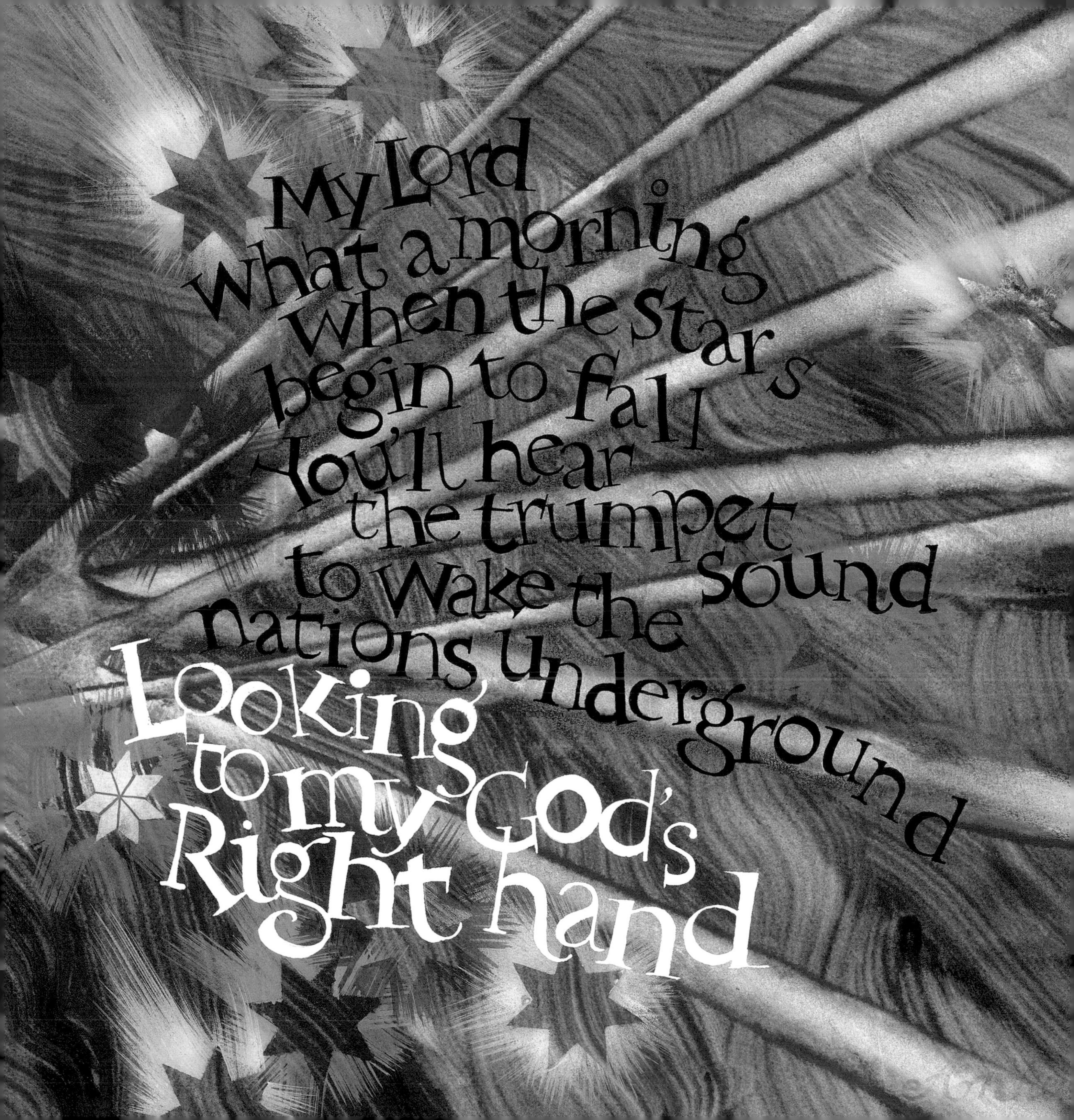

My Lord
What a morning
When the stars
begin to fall
You'll hear
the trumpet
to wake the sound
nations underground
Looking
to my God's
Right hand

In That Great Gettin' Up Morning

I'm goin' to tell you about the coming of the Savior,
Fare you well, fare you well.
There's a better day a-comin'
Fare you well, fare you well.

That the time shall be no longer . . .
For the Judgment Day is comin' . . .

The Lord spoke to Gabriel: . . .
"Blow your trumpet, Gabriel" . . .

"Lord, how loud shall I blow it?" . . .
"Loud as seven peals of thunder" . . .

Then you'll see poor sinners risin' . . .
Then you'll see the world on fire . . .

Then you'll see the Christians risin' . . .
Then you'll see the righteous marchin' . . .

See them marchin' home to heaven . . .
There they live with God forever . . .

In that great gettin' up morning
Fare you well, fare you well.
In that great gettin' up morning
Fare you well, fare you well.

It will happen in a moment, in the blink of an eye,
when the last trumpet is blown. For when the
trumpet sounds, those who have died will be raised
to live forever. And we who are living will
also be transformed. 1 CORINTHIANS 15:52

HELL
TRUMPET, GABRIEL

SEE THE RIGHTEOUS MARCHIN'

MANY DAYS IS COMIN'

YOU WELL

HOW LOUD SHALL I BLOW IT?

I SEE THEM MARCHIN' HOME TO HEAVEN

AT GETTIN' UP MORNING

YOU WELL

IN PEALS OF THUNDER

RE THEY LIVE WITH GOD FOREVER

This spiritual reveals the heart of the believer, warning people of the coming judgment with the repeated desire that they fare well. Using the image of a bugle from the Civil War period, the whole rest of the design becomes a bold announcement.

TB

O What a Beautiful City

O what a beautiful city!
O what a beautiful city!
O what a beautiful city!
Twelve gates to the city!
Hallelu!

Three gates in the east,
Three gates in the west,
Three gates in the north,
Three gates in the south,
Making it twelve gates to the city.
Hallelu!

Never been

Off their plantation, nor allowed to

Stand by the gate or get close to

Even saying I might leave here

One day. But at night

I sing a song

About Heaven and the

Twelve pretty gates up there that

Never will close to me

Because my ticket is

Paid for already

By Jesus.

PR

The holy city, Jerusalem, . . . shone with the glory of God and sparkled like a precious stone. . . .
The city wall was broad and high, with twelve gates. REVELATION 21:10-12

Come and Go with Me

Come and go with me to my Father's house,
To my Father's house, to my Father's house.
Come and go with me to my Father's house;
There is joy, joy, joy.

Jesus will be there in my Father's house, . . .

Come just as you are to my Father's house, . . .

There's music everywhere in my Father's house, . . .

People have no fear in my Father's house, . . .

Pictures of homes in Burkina Faso, covered with patterns, inspired this design for the Father's house. Do you see the people of various shades marching together inside? Jesus has promised us a future home without grief, cost, pretention, restrictions, hunger, or fear! The wonder of heaven cuts loose my imagination.

TB

You love him even though you have never seen him. Though you do not see him now, you trust him; and you rejoice with a glorious, inexpressible joy. 1 PETER 1:8

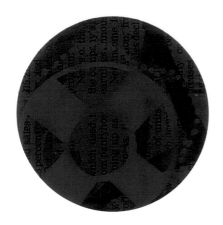

The unrelenting daily news from the wires and the press has us all on edge and in a discouraged state about humankind. So how sincere and true are the words of this spiritual that affirm the good news that we have a Savior from all oppression and sorrow. This verse puts into perspective that our time of suffering is temporary—the Kingdom is eternal!

TB

Ain't That Good News

I've got a crown in the Kingdom,
Ain't that good news?
I've a crown up in the Kingdom,
Ain't that good news?

I'm going to lay down this world,
I'm going to shoulder up my cross.
I'm going to take it home to Jesus,
Ain't that good news?

I've got a harp in the Kingdom,
Ain't that good news? . . .

I've got a robe in the Kingdom,
Ain't that good news? . . .

I've got a Savior in the Kingdom,
Ain't that good news? . . .

When the Great Shepherd appears, you will receive a crown of never-ending glory and honor. 1 PETER 5:4

Ain't that good news

I've got a crown in the Kingdom
I've got a harp in the Kingdom
I've got a robe in the Kingdom

I'm going to lay down this world
I'm going to shoulder up my cross
I'm going to take it home to Jesus

I'm going

I've got a Savior in the Kingdom

i GOT SHOES. YOU got shoes
ALL GOD'S ChiLDReN got SHOES
WHeN i GeT to HeAveN GONNA PUT ON MY shoes
i'M GONNA WALK ALL oveR GOD'S HeAveN
eveRYBODY TALkin' About heaven ain't
GOiN' tHERE

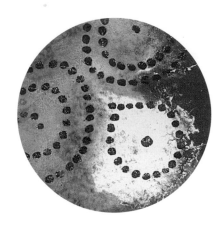

All God's Children Got Shoes

I got shoes, you got shoes,
All God's children got shoes.
When I get to heaven, gonna put on my shoes.
I'm gonna walk all over God's heaven, heaven, heaven.
Everybody talkin' about heaven ain't goin' there.
Heaven, heaven,
Gonna walk all over God's heaven.

I got a robe, you got a robe . . .

I got a crown, you got a crown . . .

I got a harp, you got a harp . . .

I got wings, you got wings . . .

Long walk in the heat

On bare feet

This blessed morning.

So I'm singing

About the glory and honor

And comforting power of

Owning and wearing and

Walking around heaven

In a glowing pair

Of brand-new

Wing tips.

PR

How beautiful on the mountains are the feet of the messenger who brings good news,
the good news of peace and salvation, the news that the God of Israel reigns! ISAIAH 52:7

King Jesus rides on a milk white horse
The River of Jordan He did cross
When I get to Heaven gonna wear a robe
Gonna see King Jesus sittin' on the throne

RIDE ON KING JESUS

No man can hinder me
Gonna walk all over those streets of gold
Goin to a land where I'll never grow old

Ride On, King Jesus

One of the most festive images of transportation from the nineteenth century is the carousel horse, the source of inspiration for this setting of the spiritual. It is a great picture of the triumph that was foreshadowed on Palm Sunday, but will be realized in the heavenly city.

TB

Ride on, King Jesus
No man can hinder me
Ride on King Jesus, ride on
No man can hinder me

King Jesus rides on a milk white horse . . .
The River of Jordan He did cross . . .

If you want to find your way to God . . .
The gospel highway must be trod . . .

When I get to Heaven gonna wear a robe . . .
Gonna see King Jesus sittin' on the throne . . .

Gonna walk all over those streets of gold . . .
Goin' to a land where I'll never grow old . . .

Then I saw heaven opened, and a white horse was standing there. Its rider was named
Faithful and True, for he judges fairly and wages a righteous war. REVELATION 19:11

When the Saints Come Marchin' In

Proud people can't march

Up there. Lying people can't

Walk up there.

Shameless people can't

Step in there.

Unholy people can't

Bribe their way into

The city whose saints

Serve and worship

And lift their voices all day,

Worshiping the God whose

Counting book

Knows our real names.

PR

When the saints come marchin' in,
When the saints come marchin' in,
Lord, I want to be in that number
When the saints come marchin' in.

When they crown Him Lord of all . . .

When they gather 'round the throne . . .

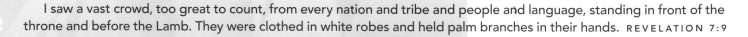

I saw a vast crowd, too great to count, from every nation and tribe and people and language, standing in front of the throne and before the Lamb. They were clothed in white robes and held palm branches in their hands. REVELATION 7:9

You can hinder me here
but you can't hinder me there

free at last

The Lord in Heaven's
goin' to answer my prayer

free at last

I went in the valley
but I didn't go to stay

Thank God Almighty

My soul get happy
and I stayed all day

I'm free at last

Free at Last

Free at last, free at last,
Thank God Almighty, I'm free at last.
Free at last, free at last,
Thank God Almighty, I'm free at last.

You can hinder me here,
But you can't hinder me there.
The Lord in Heaven's
Goin' to answer my prayer.

I went in the valley,
But I didn't go to stay.
My soul got happy,
And I stayed all day.

Can you imagine the joy of being freed from slavery? The same experience comes from Christ setting us free from the bondage of our wrongdoing. In both cases, it is the knowledge of freedom we celebrate, but the full experience comes in heaven, for which we long. I designed the broken letter style here to visually capture that wonderful release.

TB

So now there is no condemnation for those who belong to Christ Jesus. ROMANS 8:1

SCRIPTURE INDEX

IMAGE CREDITS